I0224708

A commentary on the 17th chapter
of the Gospel of John

The

Lord's

Prayer

This is not the prayer we were
taught

By Timothy White Sr.

The Lord's Prayer, A Commentary on John Chapter 17 © 2016 by Timothy White, Sr.

All rights reserved. Printed in the United States of America. No part of this book may be used or reproduced in any manner whatsoever without written permission except in the case of brief quotations embodied in critical articles or reviews.

This book is a work of non-fiction. However, names, characters, businesses, organizations, places, events and incidents either are the product of the author's imagination or are used fictitiously. Any resemblance to actual persons, living or dead, events, or locales is entirely coincidental.

**For information contact:
info@uptownmediaventures.com**

Book and Cover design by Tim White Publishing

ISBN: 978-1-68121-108-4

10 9 8 7 6 5 4 3 2 1

Table of Contents

Introduction

There are numerous prayers that fill the scriptures, and books have been written about many of them and the importance of praying. It's been said that prayer is effective, and that every religion believes in prayer, and use prayer to talk to their deity.

Prayer can be seen as cultural, as much as it is seen as individual and personal. But one thing is certain, prayer is a matter of faith by all those who practice it.

The need to pray is built into each of us, but whether or not we do so is a choice that becomes personal, and is often based on the experiences of the individual faced with a particular situation(s).

Prayer is connection to what we believe is unknown, (*outside our understanding*) and unseen by the natural eyes, God.

God is the power that is greater than man; the power that is not limited to the physical realm. God is seen as being everywhere, and has the ability to do anything.

From culture to culture, He is called by many names, but there is only one true and living God. The name He is called from one culture to another varies; the language differs from country to country and the name each calls out to the Lord appears to change, but that is not ours to judge.

In fact, there are thousands of names given to God. But each of them only describes his nature, in responds to individual needs.

When we pray, we do so, based on our specific needs and experiences in our lives. For example, here are a few names God is called: Elohim (God)

Yahweh (Lord, Jehovah)

El Elyon (The Most High God)

Adonai (Lord, Master)

El Shaddai (Lord God Almighty)

El Olam (The Everlasting God)

Jehovah Jireh (The Lord Will Provide)

Jehovah Rapha (The Lord Who Heals You)

Jehovah Nissi (The Lord Is My Banner)

El Qanna (Jealous God)

Jehovah Mekoddishkem (The Lord Who Sanctifies You)

Jehovah Shalom (The Lord Is Peace)

Jehovah Sabaoth (The Lord of Hosts)

Jehovah Raah (The Lord Is My Shepherd)

Jehovah Tsidkenu (The Lord Our
Righteousness)

Jehovah Shammah (The Lord Is There)

These are only a few names from the bible.
(***not what other cultures call Him***).

The Filipino Catholics and other Christians use
Maykapal (Creator)

In Arabic he is called Allah—meaning "the
god"

Mandaeans believe in one God, called Hayyi
Rabbi (The Great Life or The Great Living God).

Jesus once said, many sheep I have that are not
of this fold (Jewish) but they would also hear His
voice and follow Him.

John, one of the 12 disciples came to Jesus
saying that there was a man doing miracles in His
name, but was not following them (*literally*), John
said they told Him to stop, Jesus told John to leave
Him alone, He was doing what He was called of God
to do (***Luke 9: 49, 50***).

Because someone is not walking as we think
they should, or doing what we believe they ought to
be doing, does not mean they are doing wrong in the
eyes of God, so it is, also with prayer.

Prayer is interpersonal and private
communication with God. It is not always done for
the benefit of those listening to it, who just happens

to be present at the time. It is personal, sometimes private, but direct communing with God.

One of the greatest prayers in the bible is that of Jesus to His father in the book of John. Together, we will take a closer look at what I believe is truly the Lord's prayer and why.

This prayer is one of the many prayers by Jesus that was public. It was personal, but it was not private, as the disciples were present with Him as He prayed. Unlike the prayer that was to follow in the garden. That prayer would be a very private prayer, and the disciples would be asked to watch with Him, as He prayed a short distance away from them (*Matthew 26: 36-39*).

In the garden prayer Jesus would lift up, it was a private prayer, with no audience other than His Father and the Holy angels.

Now, Let's take a closer look at this, The Lord's Prayer.

17: 1

These words spake Jesus and lifted up His eyes to Heaven and said, Father, the hour is come; glorify thy Son that thy Son also may glorify thee

These are the words that Jesus spoke lifting up His eyes to Heaven, speaking directly to his Father saying, the hour is come (*17: 1*). What hour is this Jesus was referring to? Throughout His ministry, He was found saying, His time or hour was not yet, (*John 2: 4*), Jesus was referring to His being messiah, and THE ATONEMENT FOR SIN, had not yet come.

Earlier, John spoke of a time when the people sought to take Jesus and kill Him for His teaching, but it was not His hour to die, (*John 7: 27-30*). Once again, the Jews wanted to put Jesus to death, this time for His teaching when he said, He and God are in union as one (*John 8: 13-27*).

The hour spoken of Here, is the hour that Jesus was preparing for all His earthly life, and God voiced His approval to His only begotten Son for His love for this world, (*John 12: 24-28*).

It was during the feast of the Passover that Jesus let His disciples know that His hour, (*of death for sin*), was at hand (*John 13: 1*).

Jesus compares what He was about to do, to a woman who is about to give birth, and how painful it is during that time of birth, but also how quickly she forgets about the pain for the joy that immediately replaces the birth, (*John 16: 20, 21*).

Jesus wanted his disciples to know that they will have a time of sorrow, (*at His death*), but it will quickly be replaced with joy (*after His resurrection*). But there would be first a time of fear that would overtake all of them (*16: 32, 33*).

We have learned from scripture that to everything there is a season and a time to every purpose under the Heaven (*Ecclesiastes 3: 1*).

Jesus was now on the road that was leading to Calvary, His hour had come, and He asks His Father to glorify, *dox-ad-zo,* (*praise, honor, to esteem glorious*), His Son, His only begotten son (*Joh .1: 14; 18; 3: 16, 18; Acts 13: 33*).

The Sons relationship to the Father is unique. It's one that is eternal. It was said that this fellowship extends beyond the angels who were created being, Christ was in eternity with God (*Genesis 1:1; John 1: 1-12*).

Christ was not a created being, but the creator. Christ took on human nature, and became the only begotten Son of God, named Jesus.

Who being the brightness of his glory, and the express image of his person, and upholding all things by the word of his power, when he had by himself purged our sins, sat down on the right hand of the Majesty on high:

Being made so much better than the angels, as he hath by inheritance obtained a more excellent name than they.

For unto which of the angels said he at any time, Thou art my Son, this day have I begotten thee? And again, I will be to him a Father, and he shall be to me a Son?

And again, when he bringeth in the firstbegotten into the world, he saith, And let all the angels of God worship him. **Hebrews 1: 3- 6**

Jesus did not seek to glorify Himself but asked that the Father glorify Him. This is seen also in the book of Hebrews. S*o also Christ glorified not himself to be made an high priest; but he that said unto him, Thou art my Son, to day have I begotten thee.-* **Hebrews 5: 5** God ordained Jesus to become King and priest. The High Priest had to make an offering for himself before he could make the sacrifice for the people. The position of High Priest was one of humility as he represented the people before God.

Christ demonstrated humility being obedient and dying on the cross, (**Philippians 2: 8**) and becoming the lamb that was slain (**Revelation 5: 12**).

Jesus went into prayer not only as the High Priest who lifts up the offering to God, but Jesus himself, was also the offering being lifted up. *And I, if I be lifted up from the earth, will draw all men unto me. -John 12: 32*

Jesus would be glorified in two ways: one as the intercessory Priest and second as the offering that would satisfy God's need for the atonement for man's sin.

Now I know there are those who say that Jesus could not be seen as a Priest because He was not of the priestly tribe which was the tribe of Levi (*Leviticus 3: 1-10*), and Jesus was of the tribe of Judah (*Hebrews 7: 14; Revelation 5: 5*).

Jesus was a Judean (*Matthew 2: 1-6*) by natural linage by way of Joseph, who was a son (descendant of David) **Matthew 1: 20; Luke 3: 23-32.**

Son of = descendant of. Jesus was called the son of David (*Matthew 15: 22; 20: 30; 21: 9; Luke 18: 38; John 7: 42*).

The office of the Priesthood of Christ transcends the understanding of man. He is called a Priest forever after the order of Melchisedec (*Hebrews 5: 6*). This priesthood was not on the earthly level but the spiritual level (*Hebrews 7: 1-28*), as Christ priesthood was not like any before or like any to come.

Jesus is the eternal Priest that is seated at the right hand of the Father interceding for us as priest and brother. Jesus was offering up Himself to the Father as the greatest and last sacrifice.

Jesus asked His Father to glorify Him, and that the Son may glorify Him (in return).

This is the bond that ran from eternity to eternity.

17:2, 3

As thou hast given Him power over all flesh, that He should give eternal life to as many as thou has given Him.

And this is life eternal, that they might know thee the only true God, and Jesus Christ whom thou hast sent.

What is the purpose of this glorifying Jesus spoke of? It was to show that, He had been given power over all flesh as He had demonstrated by His Healing the sick, feeding the multitudes, casting out demons and even raising the dead.

All these things were great signs, miracles and wonders. But the sick did not go away, the multitudes hungered again, demons continued to oppress the world, and those raised from the dead would soon die once again.

Jesus, the son of Joseph and Mary had to be given power over eternal life. Here Jesus prays to the Father, thanking God for giving Him, (*Jesus*), the power to give eternal life, a matter that goes back to His time as Christ in Eternity.

Jesus in these verses highlights what He came to do, and that was to give eternal (*everlasting*) life. This was part of His conversation with Nicodemus, that brought about confusion to a man who was considered scholarly (***John 3: 3***).

Eternal life did not come by way of any of the many things, (*works*), that men have done, or could do (***Ephesians 2: 8, 9***).

Jesus was actively praying for those who He had chosen and was walking with Him. But His prayer would extend far beyond the 12 disciples. This prayer is inclusive and would incorporate all those who would believe later, in the days, years, and generations to come.

Jesus prayed that He should give eternal life to as many as the Father has given to Him.

And this is **eternal life** (*v.3*), the life that filled the ministry of Jesus. This life Jesus spoke of, was salvation from all that sin produced at the fall of man. In these verses, we have Jesus speaking of "they". It refers to everyone that comes to know Him, (*God the Father*) through what Jesus the Christ of God had done.

The mission of Jesus was clear, which was to get the world to honor the Father and all He had done, and this can only be achieved by accepting the Son whom the Father had sent in His name. In order to accept the Father, the world would have to embrace the Son.

Everything Jesus did, including the teaching, the miracles, healing the sick and raising the dead, reflected the Father.

Jesus was a living example of the power, the purpose and the presence of God when He said, *let your light so shine before men that they might see your good work and glorify your Father which is in Heaven* (***Matthew 5: 16***).

We must remember that God was in Christ reconciling the world unto Himself (***II Corinthians 5: 19***).

Christ came to introduce the world to God the Father as the only true and living God. Remember that no man has seen God at anytime, the only begotten Son which is in (*from the bosom, presence*) of the Father, **He** (Jesus) has declared Him (*made Him known, visible*) **John 1: 18**.

Here is where we can find life eternal. It is in knowing there is only one true God and accepting Jesus as the one who God has sent in His name to represent Him. This is only a portion of the Lord's prayer. Only a small aspect of this wonderful prayer.

17:4

I have glorified thee on earth: I have finished the work which thou gavest me to do

As Jesus continues His prayer to the Father, He lets us know that He had glorified, (*honored*) the Father on earth.

How was this done? He had finished the work His Father had given Him to do.

This was done in past, present and future tense.

Finished here, does not mean in totality, but up to a specific point, as we hear Jesus dying on the cross say, it is finished, (***John 19: 30***).

The finish spoken of here, was letting the world know and see that He was indeed the Son of God; it was the demonstration of being one with the Father that He had finished proving.

Jesus had effectively lived the life of the Lamb of God; He had been faithful to His Father. And He had completed the work that His Father had given Him to do.

Jesus' disciples on one occasion had asked Him to show them the Father and they would be satisfied. What Jesus instead tells them is this, they had already seen the Father in Him (***John 14: 8, 9***).

Jesus had effectively glorified His Father's name. And finished the work He was given to do by Him, but it does not end with this statement.

17: 5

And now O Father, glorify thou me with thy own self with the glory which I had with thee before the world was

And now Jesus goes on to say to God (*Elohim*), O Father, glorify thou me with the glory they had shared before the world was.

Here Jesus was talking about Himself as being eternal, not being a created being as some would contend; He was not an angel who was created to please and serve God.

Angels were above man in creation, but Christ did not come to earth as an angel. Christ took on human flesh as a man. He was made a little lower than the angels for the suffering of death (*Hebrews 2: 9*). The angels could not die for man or redeem him back to God.

Jesus was putting the definite article on what He was saying here. Jesus was not asking to be placed in the status of all other creation, which would be impossible since He was also the Creator. He was in the world and the world was created by Him (*John 1:10*), all things were made by Him (*John 1: 3*). So that which is created can never become the creator, but only a reproducer of what already exists.

Christ, (*not Jesus*), was always equal to the Father as seen in the book of Genesis where it is said, in the beginning God (*Elohim*) created the Heaven and the earth, (***Genesis 1:1***). The verse of particular interest is verse 26a where God is speaking says, let *us* make man in *our* own image, after *our* own likeness.

Who is the "us" referred to in this passage of scripture? Was God speaking alone or were there others with Him?

Let us look briefly at God's order of things as it might help us understand what was being said.

Before there was anything there was God. Not God plus, just God. But as we speak of God it is necessary to understand that means Elohim. Now this is where many of us as human beings living in natural bodies have difficulty understanding God.

The bible tells us that the natural man receives not the things of God, neither can he know, (*understand*) them because they are spiritually discerned (***I Corinthians 2: 14***). Even being born again, is not a guarantee that we will grasp it, since this comes only in God's time, and it will serve His purpose.

Before there was anything created there was three that existed. The Father, the Word and the Spirit (***I John 5: 7***).

It was Elohim God that created all that is.

Before God created man He created the angels, so they existed before man. God created the heavens and the earth.

After God had created the heavens and the earth, we find the six days of creation. Christ was not a part of creation, He was the creator. Jesus, (*the*) Christ, the same yesterday, today, and forever (*Hebrews 13: 8*).

It was this glory, that Jesus was referring to in His prayer, that He shared with His Father before anything existed.

Notice that the word "I" is used often in this chapter, in fact it is used more than 30 times, showing its intimacy with its intended recipient.

17: 6

I have manifested thy name unto the men which thou gavest me out of the world: thine they were, and thou gavest them me, and they have kept thy word.

Jesus goes on to say that He had manifested His name (**God the Father**) to the men He (**God the Creator**) had given to Him (Jesus) out of the world.

They were God's by creation and Christs' by new birth.

It is here that we see that God is supremely sovereign and knows all things. Each of them was chosen by God. In fact, they were chosen in Christ before the foundation of the world (*Ephesians.1: 4*).

All that Jesus did was inclusive and the words He spoke here was active. In other words, they had more than just the men who traveled with Jesus in mind, and would also include all who would come to believe and accept Jesus as their savior. It is clear from these words that God knows who will be saved.

Since God is sovereign and knows all before it takes place, then what is the purpose of salvation? Salvation restores the line that was broken in the garden; it puts man back on track to obey God without the excuse of sin.

It is God's way of letting us know that we can serve, love and obey Him in these earthly bodies, because He has shown us the way through His Son Jesus.

God has put up a caution sign, and here it is. He knows who will be saved, its called predestination, (*Ephesians 1: 5*). Jesus chose the disciples, but He also knew and knows the hearts of all men (*Jeremiah 17: 9, 10; John 2: 24, 25*).

Here's something else we need to know about predestination. It falls under what we call **the divine will of God**. God is sovereign and omnipotent, and you and I are not.

God knows who will be saved, you and I do not.

God is not willing that any should perish, but all come to repentance, (*II Peter 3: 9*). God has chosen the foolishness of preaching to save mankind (*I Corinthians 1: 21*). The preaching of the cross is foolishness to those who are perishing (*I Corinthians 1: 18*).

Here's something the Saints need to know today. Since we are not God, we do not know who will be saved, so it's our responsibility to follow the great commission given by the Lord, (*Matthew 28: 19, 20*).

We are not to spend our time trying to say who is saved, and who is not, only God knows. That falls under what **I call, none of our business**. Let's be mindful to remember that salvation is personal between that individual and God.

We are not to spend God's precious time in judgment over anyone's salvation. The Holy Spirit will deal with all such matters (*John 16: 7-15*).

Salvation is not from us, but God, in the morning sow your seeds, in the evening withhold not your hand (*Ecclesiastes 11: 6*) we do not know what will grow and what will not grow. That is in God's hands.

Paul put it this way to the Corinthian church: I have planted, Apollos watered, but God gave the increase (*I Corinthians 3: 6*). Paul goes on to say that neither he that plants is anything, (special), nor is the person that waters anything (special), but God gives the increase (*v. 7*). The important thing was what God did, and that was to save souls.

Jesus had declared the Father's name to those who were given to Him out of the world. These were men selected by God and given to Christ for the ministry.

But what did Jesus mean when He said they had kept God's word? It could not mean that they had kept the words of Jesus as they were not empowered yet by the Holy Spirit.

The key Here is, they **"kept thy word"**, each of them, as Jews were practicing their faith in God by keeping the Commandments, (*as best they could*), as well as the Passover.

The disciples were young in the faith and teachings of Jesus. They were yet under the old covenant. It would not be until after Jesus' death and resurrection that they would move into the new covenant that He had spoken about in the upper room, (*Matthew 26: 28*). The disciples had kept the Laws, thus the Commandments.

17: 7

Now they have known that all things whatsoever thou hast given me are of thee

Even now, Jesus goes on to say the disciples have known that all things, that they had seen, heard, and been a part of, came from God.

Look at something John would later write to reflect what Jesus said: that which was from the beginning, which we (*The disciples*) have seen with our eyes, which we have looked upon, and our hands have handled of the word of life, (*for the life was manifested, and we have seen it, and bear witness, and show unto you that eternal life, which was with the Father, and manifested unto us*), that which we have seen and heard declare we unto you, that you also may have fellowship with us: and truly our fellowship is with the Father, and with His Son Jesus Christ (*I John 1: 1-3*).

Jesus was the only person who could truly keep the Commandments of God. Everyone born violated the Commandments of God until Jesus came into the world. The Commandments pointed to Christ; it was the schoolmaster until Christ came (*Galatians 3: 24, 25*).

The Law was a shadow of things to come. It did not make anyone sinless and offerings had to be continued year to year (*Hebrews 10:1-3*).

The bible is about man's relationship to God, as Jesus prayer is also about that same relationship. Its emphasis is on knowing God and our fellowship with Him.

Jesus came to restore that covenant relationship and fellowship that had been broken through sin.

17: 8

For I have given unto them the words which thou gavest me; and they have received them, and have known surely that I came from thee, and they have believed that thou didst send me.

I have given them the words you have given me Jesus says. He did not want any confusion as to what He was doing here on earth. He did not come seeking glory for Himself.

Jesus came Here out of obedience to God to take away sin (*John 1:29*), becoming the perfect sacrifice for sin, saying, I come in the volume of the book as it is written of me, to do your will O God (*Hebrews 10:7*).

When Jesus was raised from the dead, we are told He opened the disciples understanding and began to relate to them from the word of God, all those things that pertained to Him, in the Law of

Moses, in the prophets, and in the Psalms concerning Him (*Luke 24: 44, 45*).

The message of Jesus was a divine lesson from God. Everything Jesus did was pointing to the Father as the one who sent Him, and everything He did was authorized by God Himself.

All the trouble that Jesus experienced from man was due to His claim that He and God were one; that He worked in perfect harmony with God; that His words were God's, and that His actions were directed by God.

His prayer was to encourage the disciples to continue to believe all that they had witnessed in His life.

Jesus thanks the Father for their faith, because the disciples received the words that Jesus had spoken to them, but also believed that not only the words came from God, but that Jesus himself also proceeded from God (*John 8: 42*).

Salvation was not in the words written, but rather in the faith to accept them as a promise from God, as is seen in the book of Romans. That if you shall confess with your mouth the Lord Jesus, and believe in your Heart that God has raised Him from the dead, thou shall be saved. For with the Heart, (*mind, conscience, will*) man believes unto righteousness, and with the mouth confession is made unto salvation, (*Romans 10: 9, 10*).

Jesus is thanking His father for their, (our) salvation.

17: 9

I pray for them: I pray not for the world, but for them which thou hast given me; for they are thine.

Jesus continues His prayer saying He was not praying for the world, but rather for His disciples. Why did he do that? We have learned that the whole world lies in wickedness (*I John 5: 19*), there is wickedness in man (*Romans 1: 18-32*).

Jesus said if we were of the world the world would love its own, but the world would reject us because Jesus had chosen us out of the world (*John 15: 19*).

Jesus loved His own who were in the world (*John 13: 1*), but in the world, does not mean of the world, (*I John 2: 15-17*).

This does not mean that we are to be so heavenly minded, that we do not fulfill the will of God for our lives while we journey here on earth. We have to live here, but we should do so as strangers and pilgrims, (*I Peter 2: 11*), knowing this is not our home.

We are renters, not owners. In other words, we must be ready and willing to leave everything behind, if the Lord requests so. No man is worthy if he puts his hand to the plow then turns to go back Jesus said, (*Luke 9: 57-62*).

Jesus said with certainty, that no man can serve two masters, (*Matthew 6: 24; Luke 16: 13*), we cannot serve God and mammon, (*money, material possessions*).

To be a friend to the world is to be an enemy towards God (*James 4: 4*).

Jesus' prayer was for the protection of those who He had called from the world. The Holy Spirit would be our guide as we navigate our way through this life.

We must trust in the Lord with all our Hearts, and lean not unto our own understanding. We must acknowledge Him (God) in all our ways, and He will direct our path (*Proverbs 3: 5, 6*).

The world is not going to change. It is what it is, filled with darkness. The believer's focus should be on individuals. Our lives are filled with only one mission for God, and that is to share His word with the lost.

There is no greater strength and power than to know that the High Priest Jesus Christ has prayed for us.

17: 10

And all mine is thine and thine is mine; and I am glorified in them.

Jesus said that He gives His sheep eternal life, and they shall never perish, neither shall any man pluck them out of His hand (*care*), but the Father who gave us to Jesus was greater than all, (*situations, circumstances, adversities*), and no man is able to pluck us from the Fathers hand (*John 10:28, 29*).

All that Jesus had belonged to God, and all that God has, is in our Lord's hands. Jesus put it this way: *I and my Father are one* (*John 10: 30*). In the future tense Jesus said, He is glorified in them, meaning every believer through all generations.

Everyone who has sold out for Jesus is known by their fruit, both the fruit of their labor, as well as the fruit of the Holy Spirit.

Believers are to bear fruit (*John 15:1-8*), and there should be results (proof) of our salvation in what we do, as well as the fruits of the Holy Spirits abiding presence, changing us from the inside out (*Galatians 5: 22, 23*).

Jesus in this verse said, he is glorified, (honored) in the life of the believers or saints. God placed the baton of faith in Jesus Christ hands. And when Christ ascended back to

Heaven, he placed that baton in the Holy Spirit works, and the Holy Spirit by faith has made each believer a walking living baton of faith in Christ.

17: 11

And now I am no more in the world, but these are in the world, and I come to thee. Holy Father, keep through thine own name those whom thou hast given me, that they may be one, as we are.

I am no longer in the world. Jesus' sights were no longer fixed on the things that would pertain to this world. He had called the men that His Father had chosen in Him from before the foundation of the world.

Jesus had spent time teaching them the ways of God. Jesus the person, the Lamb of God, loved His disciples and even as He was preparing to leave them, prayed for them, knowing what they were soon to be faced with.

It would not be easy for any of them. They would be marked men for their faith and fellowship with Christ, (*Matthew 26: 69-74; Mark 14:66-72*).

Later, after Jesus' resurrection and ascension, there would be trouble for all the early believers, most notably from one man, Saul of Tarsus (*Acts 9: 1, 2*).

The saints would suffer many horrible deaths at the hands of an unbelieving world.

Jesus' prayer was for those who were being left in this sinful and evil world. It was expedient that Jesus goes back to the Father. He said this was important, and He had to do so, that the third person of the Godhead could come to them, in the person of the Holy Spirit (*John 16: 7*).

Can you hear the intensity of Jesus' prayer? **Holy Father** keep through your own name (*power)* those who are given to me Jesus ask.

Jesus' request was that they, we, all believers, experience what it is like to be one with God, what a perfect union and harmony that will be.

This line of Jesus' prayer is that all believers become one in faith he said, as he and the Father were. This would be important as they would need one another, when the time of trials and tribulations come from the unbelieving world.

17: 12

While I was with them in the world I kept them in thy name: those that thou gavest me I kept, and none of them is lost, but the son of perdition that the scripture might be fulfilled.

Jesus' mission on earth was not only to come and die for man's sin, but also to teach those selected by God to go and teach that God had given a propitiation for sin in His Son Jesus.

That there would no longer be a need for goats, doves, or sheep. God has satisfied Himself with the ultimate offering in His Son.

Salvation is from God the Father through His Son Jesus Christ. Throughout Jesus' ministry, He was always pointing His disciples to the fact that He was in relationship to the Father. Every step along the way to the cross Jesus spoke constantly of His Father.

The people had become blind to who God is, (*John 9: 39-41*). Man's relationship with God suffered because of their sin, and over time, man went about doing what was right in His own eyes, as we see when there was no King in Israel, (*Judges 17: 6*).

Israel had backslidden and did not do as the Lord had commanded them (*Hosea 11: 7*) and they were called foolish people who had no understanding, which had eyes and see not and which had ears that hear not (*Jeremiah 5: 21*).

The Lord said He would heal Israel's backsliding one day and would freely love them and His anger would be turned away from them (*Hosea 14: 4*).

Rome was ruling over Israel and the religious rulers of the day were given limited powers as they pleased Caesar.

The Jews were permitted to keep their religious ceremonies and Commandments from their God, as long as it did not interfere with the operations of Rome.

It was not uncommon for Rome to have spies who were keeping an eye on the inner workings of the Jews. And their religion.

Such a case can be found in some of those who came to the trial of Jesus and gave a false testimony concerning some of the things He had said, (*Matthew 26: 59-61*). Compare what was really said (*John 2: 19*).

In the Psalms, we find the words, my enemies speak evil of me. When shall He die, and His name perish? (*Psalm 41: 5*) and again it was said, all that hate me whisper together against me: against me to do me hurt (*v. 7*)

The first part of the disciples, (Apostles) mission was to get the word to the lost sheep of the house of Israel (*Matthew 10: 5, 6*).

It is here that the Prayer of Jesus is fixed. These men were all Jews, who were handpicked, yet there seemed to be one person who seemed not to belong.

Christ had kept the Father's name lifted up before the disciples. Everyone seemed to be on board with keeping the word of God as taught by Jesus, all but one. How could that be when He was one of the men chosen by Jesus?

Jesus at the supper table, let the disciples know that it would be one of them sitting at the table, whose hand was also on the table that would betray Him, (*Matthew 26:21-23*).

Prophecy says, it would be one who was seen as a friend, (*Psalm 41: 9*). But even more than that, it would be one who was a disciple.

Let's understand something about this word disciple. Just because one is called a disciple, does not mean they are a believer.

A disciple is a student or learner, of another's teachings and principles. This does not mean they share their belief.

A disciple can accept a teaching but not accept the teacher. Jesus was not the first teacher or Rabbi to have disciples.

Moses had disciples, Aaron, Hur and Joshua was some of Moses disciples. John the Baptist had disciples (*John 1: 35*), and of course Jesus had disciples (*Luke 9: 1*).

What is this about the one who is called the son of perdition, *Apoleia* (*destruction, ruin, loss*)? How could such a person become a disciple?

Here is what you and I must consider, and that is, everyone who hears the word of God is not going to accept it. Why they reject the word of God is unknown, at least to us, and on this earthly level.

As we said earlier, God is sovereign. What Judas would do he had already purposed in his own Heart to do in spite of what Jesus would say or do. (*I speak more on this in the book, **The truth was revealed in the upper room***).

Does this mean it is useless to worship or even serve God since there are people who it appears are destined to go to hell, and why even bother to read the bible, or make a confession?

We confess because it is the Holy Spirit who is speaking to us, just as Judas was given chances to make the right decision, he with conscious intent and purpose chose to reject God.

Could Judas have changed his mind anywhere along the course? It is possible but not likely he would have done so. Judas had his own agenda. Jesus said have I not chosen you twelve and yet one of you is a devil, *deceiver, pretender* (*John 6: 70*).

This declaration by Jesus came as He was talking about being the bread of life, and they would have to eat of His flesh and drink of His blood to be in association with Him and the Father.

It is the Spirit that quickens (*gives life*). Jesus goes on to say, the words He spoke were spirit and they were life, but some of them believed not. Jesus said this referring to Judas and others who did not or would not believe (***John 6: 62-64***).

Look at the immediate result for some of the disciples that were following, from that time (*moment*). Many of the disciples, (*remember what we have learned about a disciple*) went back, and walked no more with Jesus.

One would remain with Jesus. He was chosen by the Lord, yet his Heart was never repentant, and that would be Judas.

Here is some food for thought. You and I would not have known this fact about Judas except the Lord revealed it in the word of God. There are many such Judas's in the world and the church today.

If the scriptures were being written today, how many people could be named just as Judas was named, that are betraying Jesus. People who are preaching in the churches, teaching Sunday school classes, calling themselves Christians, but are simply using the name of Jesus just to get their agendas across?

Jesus thanked the Father that the only one He lost as a Rabbi, a teacher, as a preacher and a leader in Israel was Judas.

All those who belong to God Jesus said, would come to Him. Judas had a title, but many are called but only a few are truly chosen, (*Matthew 20: 16*).

Was it prophecy that Judas fulfilled by his betrayal? As we have mentioned already it was **Psalms 41:9**, and it was fulfilled in the garden, when Judas lead the way for those who were to arrest Jesus. Note what it was that Jesus said to Judas when he kissed Him, *Friend, wherefore art thou come?*

In plain English Jesus said, friend why are you here? As it was said, Judas was familiar with the place that Jesus would pray regularly, (*John 18: 1-3*). Just as Judas fulfilled scripture, let us not deceive ourselves, because you and I are also fulfilling scripture as well.

17: 13

And now I come to thee. And these things I speak in the world, that they might have my joy fulfilled in themselves.

Jesus would be leaving the disciples soon. His earthly connection to them would be severed that evening, by way of fear and by the way of his impending trial and death on the cross. This would become a great time of sadness.

Jesus was on His way back to the Father. He would be leaving His teaching for them to follow. It would be the last thing on any of their mind when He is arrested later that night, but the words Jesus spoke would be stirred within them by the Holy Spirit not many days from then.

Jesus had often told the disciples to believe in Him, as they believed in the Father (*John 14: 1*). He told them that He would give them peace (*John 14: 27*), and Jesus said His joy should remain in them (*John 15: 11*).

Jesus had given them the promise of the Holy Spirit who would bring His words back to mind (*John 14:16; 16: 7-15*).

These words spoken by Jesus were to be an encouragement to the disciples of a promise to come, during the dark hours they were about to face.

It would be the Holy Spirit who would give the disciples the boldness to stand up for Jesus, and the Holy Spirit who would bring the joy of serving Christ back to the disciples. Joy is one of the attributes of the Holy Spirit (*Galatians 5:22, 23*).

The joy that Jesus referred to was not a joy that the world would or could give. The joy He spoke on was a joy that wells up and flows from inside, as He said to the woman at the well.

The joy Christ spoke of would be living waters bursting forth, springing up into everlasting life,

(*John 4: 14*). The water referred to here is the Holy Spirit, (*John 7: 38, 39*).

The Holy Spirit brings the joy of salvation through Jesus Christ the only begotten Son of God.

Salvation would be a testimony unto itself, the believers would not need to be validated by anyone, and the proof would be inside them, (*John 14: 23*).

If we receive the witness of men, the witness of God is greater: for this is the witness of God which He testified of His Son, that he that believes on the Son of God has the witness (proof) in Himself: He that believes not God has made God a liar, because He has not believed the record (evidence) that God gave His Son (*I John 5: 9, 10*).

You and I are only working out what God has worked in us. We are to work out our own salvation, with fear (*reverence*) and trembling (*caution*), as we are told (*Philippians 2: 12*).

Be very careful here! This scripture does not say you are **working for** your salvation, but rather **working out**, your salvation.

In other words, believers are to be busy going about and doing God's business, learning and sharing God's word with a lost humanity according to the great commission (*Matthew 28: 19, 20*).

The believer's assurance is in knowing that it is God who is at work in us, doing what pleases Him, (*Philippians 2: 13*).

17: 14

I have given them thy word; and the world hath hated them, because they were not of the world, even as I am not of the world.

All believers must know that there is a price for following Christ. Rest assured it would not be popular to serve Christ. The world is not friendly towards those who would keep God's word.

Jesus came to restore man's fellowship that was broken in the garden, but in doing so, He had to let man know just how sinful he truly was and remains still.

Sin is the most sensitive subject we are faced with as saints of God. Whenever sin is mentioned, it is often accompanied by those who seek to continue in their sin, usually saying, judge not lest you be judge (*Matthew 7: 7*). Or you Hear, all have sinned and come short of the glory of God (*Romans 3:23*). This is often done as a means to justify themselves.

God loves everyone, some have said, and although this is true. God does loves everyone, and He makes that very clear, (*John 3: 16*), it does not end there. The word of God also says, God is angry with the wicked every day, (*Psalm 7: 11*).

There are some who say we are all children of God, again true in part. We are all children of God through creation, but we become sons and daughters of God by the new birth (*I John 3: 1-3*).

This new birth means we are no longer friends with the world and therefore no longer in agreement with its sinfulness.

The word of God asked an important question in the book of Amos, can two walk together unless they agree? (*Amos 3: 3*)

We are told that the whole world lies in wickedness (*I John 5: 19*).

The instruction to the saints of God is this, to come out from among them (*the lost, confused and sinful*) and be separate, unto the Lord. (*II Corinthians 6: 17*)

There is none good, no, not even one person (*Psalm 14: 1-3*). Man cannot boast of his good qualities, as he has none. The good that we would do comes from God (*James 1: 17*).

As long as we do our best to fit in, the world would be very accepting of us. Just do not buck the system; do not go against the grain or what is now considered the "Norm".

To call things sin these days, is thought to be overly religious. We should be preaching the feel-good gospel, the gospel that says everything is right with the world. It is better to be friends with the world, but we are told that friendship with the world (*of sin*) is to be an enemy towards God (***James 4: 4***).

Saints are told to come out from among them (*those who practice sinning*), and to be separate, sanctified, and holy.

The world doesn't mind our being religious, everyone calls themselves religious or spiritual. It is being righteous that they have a problem with. Being religious and righteous are not the same.

17: 15

I pray not that you take them out of the world, but that thou shouldest keep them from the evil.

Jesus in this wonderful prayer to the Father does not ask His Father to after our salvation to remove the saints from the world. Jesus said that in this world we shall have tribulation (***John 16: 33***).

Why would Jesus pray that the Father leave the believers in the world, especially knowing what is in this world, and how the world treats people who call on the name of the Lord?

I know there are some believers that wish that the Lord would take them out of the world as soon as they were saved.

It would save them the Heartache of seeing those they may have wronged, or not face the sins they might have done in the course of their life.

Saints were saved and sealed for service, not to just sit around. There is much work to be done. Jesus said to the believers, pray to the Father that He would send workers into the vineyard. The harvest is plenteous (*ripe for the gospel*) but the laborers are few (***Luke 10: 2***). This is a task for workers not worriers.

There is no work we must do in heaven. It is all worship and praise there, but it is here on earth that the floodgates of sin have been opened. This is not difficult work to do. Jesus said, to take His yoke upon ourselves and learn of Him, that He is meek and lowly, (*humble*) in heart, and we shall find rest for our souls. His yoke is easy he said, and His burden is light, (***Matthew 11: 29, 30***).

Jesus' prayer to His Father was not that we should be taken away from the problems of life with all its trials; the prayer is that the saints should be kept from the evil (*one*) while journeying through this evil world. The Holy Spirit has sealed us.

This does not mean however, that we will not be attacked on every side.

Paul wrote to the Saints telling them to put on the whole armor of God, (***Ephesians 6: 10-12***), Peter said also, that our adversary the devil is like a roaring lion that goes around looking for those He can devour (*I Peter 5: 8*).

Satan attacked Peter during His hour of fleshly weakness, (*Matthew 26: 69-75*).

Jesus was not praying to the Father about tribulation. He said in this life we shall have tribulations, (*John 16: 33*), that is anguish, troubles and pain. These are things that accompany life in general. Job tells us that man is born unto trouble (*Job 5: 7*).

Jesus lets us know that God sends the rain on the just and the unjust alike (*Matthew 6: 45*)

Paul tells the believers that these natural things, (*calamities*, *adversities*), cannot separate us from the love of God that is in Christ Jesus, (*Romans 8: 35*).

This however is not what the Lord Jesus is talking about here in His prayer.

Here Jesus is speaking about the evil one, Satan and sin. He is praying about spiritual protection from the Father for his children.

We are all tempted (*James 1:13, 14*). God will not permit us to be tempted beyond what we can endure, (*I Corinthians 10: 13*).

The key here is our leaning and depending on the Lord and surrendering ourselves to the Spirit of God.

This prayer is not about natural choices, but sinful practices that are in direct opposition to the revealed word of God.

Look at some of these sins! They have nothing to do with the wind, rain, floods or storms. They are sins that come from within the minds and actions of rebellious men and women, (*Romans 1: 18-32; I Corinthians 6: 9, 10; Galatians 5: 19-21*).

All sins referenced here has to do with man's willful choice to resist God. These sins result from being led astray by the evil *one*, as Jesus was praying about. This is what He is referring to as He asks His Father to keep the believers safe.

This safety is greatest as the believers yield to the power of the Holy Spirit.

Saints do sin, but we have an advocate with the Father in the person of Jesus Christ we can go to, (*I John 2: 1*). We must confess our sins and He will cleanse us from all unrighteousness, (*I John 1: 9*).

If we are not sure what to say, God has made a provision for us in the person of the Holy Spirit. We do not know what to pray sometimes, as the words are hard to form because we can be burdened, so the Holy Spirit does a remarkable work for us, and in us, before the throne of God, and he speaks on our behalf (*Romans 8: 26*).

Was Jesus saying in this prayer that there was a possibility that the believer could be overtaken? Overtaken here means caught up in a sin. It could happen, but this does not mean they have lost their salvation, they will require help, however (*Galatians 6: 1*).

Everyone is placed in the body of Christ for what they can do to support the ministry, (*I Corinthians 12: 1-31*).

How is the Father going to keep us from the evil? John put it this way, how can you love God who you have not seen and hate your brother who you see every day (*I John 4: 40*).

Cain was asked by the Lord, where was His Brother Abel? This was after Cain had committed the first murder of another human being, his own brother, Abel. Cain's response to the Lord was, am I my brother's keeper (*Genesis 4: 9*)?

The truth is, we are our brothers keeper, again look at what John said, *we know we have passed from death unto life, because we love the brethren, He that loves not His brother abides in death, whosoever hates His brother is a murderer, and we know no murderer has eternal life abiding in Him* (*I John 3: 14, 15*).

The strength of our heavenly fellowship is directly seen by our earthly relationship with other believers, but it extends far beyond that.

Jesus said if we only love those who love us we are no different than the unregenerate, (*Matthew 5: 46-48*).

We are to be a source of strength to our brothers and sisters in the faith, but always remain a joy to God, by way of Jesus Christ. These things cannot be done unless the Lord leaves us here and allows life, situations and circumstances to challenge our faith.

We, the members and body of Christ, must submit ourselves to God. Resist the devil (*the evil*) and He will flee from us, (*James 4: 7*).

We are reminded that, greater is He, (*the Lord*) who is in us, than he, (*the evil, Satan*) that is in the world, (*I John 4: 4*).

Jesus in this prayer asks that we not be taken out of the world so that we can go through the process of spiritual growth that is needed by every believer. His prayer to the Father was to keep us, to fortify and strengthen us, and not remove us from the world's situations.

We must be like David when he asked, who is this King of Glory? The Lord strong and mighty, the Lord mighty in battle (*Psalm 24: 8*).

17:16

They are not of the world, even as I am not of the world.

In scripture it is clear who has been with Jesus. There are things that show up in a life that has been affected by the Lord.

The world is affected by Jesus one way, and those who know Him as their savior are affected yet another way.

The call of Jesus was for change, repentance and restoration. It was the call to step away from the human way of doing things and move into a higher realm.

It was time to move from focusing on materialism things, to thoughts of spiritual change.

A call from Jesus is a call to change. To answer Jesus' call, you must stop what you are doing, (*Matthew 4: 18-22; 9: 9*). This call is a call from the world to be a witness.

In this verse we hear Jesus declare that those who believe in him are not of the world, just as he was not of the world.

As born-again children of God we are told, Love not the world, neither the things that are in the world. If any man love the world, the love of the Father is not in him. (*I John 2: 15*)

As saints of God we have the victory over the world, this victory comes from our faith, the faith that comes from believing in Christ (*I John 5: 4, 5*).

The Saints of God are not bound to the world, but we are free to serve Christ in spirit and in truth, to drink from the eternal fountain of life. Those who the Son set free are free indeed, (*John 8: 36*).

17: 17

Sanctify them through thy truth, thy word is truth.

The Heart of Jesus' prayer is that the believers be sanctified, that they be set apart for God's holy purpose.

The believer is not of the world. They are being kept by the power of God the Father. Their strength is in surrendering to the Holy Spirit.

The Saints are preserved and filled with the presence of God. We have been bought with a price, (*the blood of Jesus on Calvary*) and we are not our own, (*I Corinthians 6: 19*).

Sanctification, **the act of being made holy, consecrated, set apart, made sacred, to make free from sin.**

Look at what the Apostle Paul said to the church in Corinth that takes place when someone comes to know the Lord Jesus. They are washed, they are sanctified, and they are justified by the Holy Spirit of God (*I Corinthians 6: 11*).

In the Old Testament the Lord required from Moses that all males born should be sanctified to Him, (*Exodus 13: 1, 2*).

Before the children of Israel could come before the Lord, they had to wash themselves, and sanctify themselves for three days, before presenting themselves in the presence of the Lord at the foot of Mt. Sinai, (*Exodus 19: 8-11*). What a beautiful picture of the power and majesty of God, and a picture humility and sanctification of man.

The process of sanctification was not new. The disciples were well aware of its importance.

Sanctification was not a calling out but rather a setting aside. It means one can remain in the world but set apart from it for service to the Lord. Amen.

It is Christ that leads the way in sanctification, not just here on earth but also in Heaven, being the captain of our salvation (*Hebrews 2: 10*).

The word of God is truth. Jesus rebuked Satan with the word of God telling Him that man does not live by bread alone, but by every word of God, (**Matthew 4: 4**).

The Psalmist said, thy word have I hid in my Heart that I might not sin against thee (**Psalm 119: 11**) and again said, thy word is a lamp unto my feet and a light unto my pathway, (**Psalm 119: 105**).

The known word of God referred to by Jesus is the Old Testament (*Tanakh*) and the Law (*Torah*) in particular.

It is the Law that Jesus speaks about in His Sermon on the Mount (**Matthew 5: 21, 27, 31, 33, 38, and 43**).

David prayed, *O my God, I trust in thee: let me not be ashamed, let not my enemies triumph over me, let none that wait on you be ashamed: let them be ashamed that which transgress without cause, show me thy ways O lord teach me thy path. Lead me in thy truth and teach me: for thou art the God of my salvation; on thee do I wait all the day* (**Psalm 25: 2-5**). What a practical prayer for even today's believer.

Jesus said that He is the way the truth and the life, no man comes unto the Father except by Him (**John 14: 6**). We must be sanctified.

Sanctifying is to be set apart for a special use, by the person who has made the selection, this person being God. The Father's truth is simple, Jesus Christ who God has sanctified, is also the one who sanctifies us.

17: 18

As thou hast sent me into the world, even so I have also sent them into the world.

Here now is a picture of the pending mission of the believers who is called the church. Christ was sending His disciples into the world to continue the work that He had begun. **Believers are sanctified then sent out**.

Jesus said, He that believes in Him the works that He did, they, (*the body of Christ*) would do, and even greater works because Jesus would be going back to the Father, (*John 14: 12*).

The believers would not be going into the world helpless. They would receive power when the Holy Spirit came, (*Acts 1: 8*), but they were to do nothing until that time. They were to tarry, (*wait*) in Jerusalem until they receive this anointing from God, (*Luke 24: 49*).

Theirs would be a mobile ministry. Jesus had instructed the disciples as to what they were to do in His great commission, when He said to them, *Go you therefore, and teach all nations, baptizing them in the name of the Father,, and in the name of the*

Son, and the Holy Ghost (Spirit), teaching them to observe all things whatsoever I have commanded you, and lo, I am with you always, even until the end of the world. Amen, Matthew 28: 19, 20.

Before this time everyone was baptized with the baptism of John, which **was a baptism of repentance (***Acts 18: 25; 19: 3-5***)**, in preparation for the coming Savior into the world. John's baptism was an acknowledgment that mankind needed to turn from their wicked ways and repent (*Matthew 3: 1, 2; Mark 1: 4; Luke 3: 2-18; John 1: 19-27)*).

The world would soon begin experiencing a transition, moving from law to grace (*John 1: 17*).

Jesus did not destroy the law He fulfilled it (*Matthew 5: 17*).

Before Christ came, no one kept the law (*though many have said otherwise*). This is why they had to continuously make sacrifices for sin. God could only be satisfied with a sin offering that was without sin, pure and unspotted to purge man's sins once and for all (*Numbers 28: 1-31*).

There would be no more need to do this after God accepted the offering made by His Son. Compare (*Matthew 27:51*) with *Exodus 26:31-37*.

Christ was not sending His disciples back into the world with old wine. He was putting new wine in new bottles.

The message is clear. Christ had done the work the Father had sent Him to do. Jesus now ask the Father to let that work continue as He sends a prepared people (*his disciples*) back out into the world, with the greatest message of hope that could ever be told. It was the power to tell the story of God's love, and how He has redeemed mankind back to Himself.

17: 19

And for their sakes, I sanctify myself, that they also might be sanctified through the truth.

Jesus said that no man takes his life, but that He laid it down willingly and was given the power from His Father to take it up again, (*John 10:17, 18*).

Jesus had to be willing to lay down His life. He sanctified Himself by doing so. Jesus did this for the disciples to know that they also would have the power to face whatever would come their way.

The disciples would have to drink of the baptism that Jesus drank, (*Matthew 20: 22, 23; Mark 10: 39*).

Each of them would have to walk the path that Jesus had paved before them. It would by no means be welcoming to them. It was a world that had two gates that it was offering. One path would lead to destruction and the other would lead to life (*Matthew 7: 13, 14*).

The believers would all be sanctified through the truth as it would be revealed to them by the Holy Spirit. Christ had given them the example to follow in Him.

17: 20

Neither I pray for these only alone, but for them also which shall believe on me through their word.

Jesus' love was not just for His immediate disciples, it transcends space and time, as He is the Alpha and Omega, the first and the last, the beginning and the end (*Revelation 1: 8*).

God's love would reach down through time, as the omnipotent creator. Jesus prays for all those who would believe in the ages to come, those who would believe because of their, (*the disciples*) witness, their testimony, and their word.

Jesus did not isolate the disciples; this faith would include all believers.

As Saints, we should always have other believers in our thoughts, but more than that we should have lost loved ones and friends also in our prayers, remembering that God is not willing that any should perish but all come to repentance (*II Peter 3: 9*).

The disciples came to Jesus asking Him to teach them how to pray, Jesus gave them insight as to some of the key ingredients and elements of prayer. (*Luke 11: 1-13*). This **MODEL PRAYER**, has been called the Lord's prayer. But we must ask ourselves would the Lord, the spotless lamb of God, ask to be delivered from His sins (*trespasses, wrongdoings*)? To do so is to nullify Jesus' claim to be the spotless lamb of God. The prayer Jesus taught them was a model prayer.

A sinner cannot take away sin. He can forgive those who sins against Him (*Matthew 6:14; 18: 21 22*), only God can forgive sin (*Luke 5: 21*).

Everything the believer is, rest on this, that Jesus is the final sacrifice to be accepted by God for sin. This truth is known as the gospel message, that is passed on through the power of the Holy Spirit. This was part of the prayer of Jesus for His Saints.

17: 21

That they all might be one; as thou, Father, art in me, and I in thee, that they also may be one in us: that the world may believe that thou hast sent me.

The oneness Jesus is speaking of here is that knowledge that comes from God, that there is only one Lord, one faith, and one baptism (*Ephesians 4: 5*), that there is only one God and Father of all (*v.6*).

Just as Jesus and the Father operate in harmony as one, this continued oneness is to be seen in all believers. Just as the body is one and has many members, so is the body of Christ (*I Corinthians 12*).

God is not the author of confusion and discord, (*I Corinthians 14: 33*), for where confusion is, there is every evil, (*at*) work (*James 3: 16*).

There is no schism, (division) in the body of Christ, (*I Corinthians 12: 25*).

Just as the Father sent me, even so I send you Jesus said to His disciples, and He breathed on them and told them receive the Holy Ghost, (*John 20: 21, 22*).

The Father sent the Son, the Son sent the Holy Spirit, and because the Holy Spirit is in every Saint of God, He guides us unto all good, (God's) work.

We are one with the Father and with His Son Jesus Christ.

Just as the world could see and hear the testimony of Jesus concerning His relationship, and fellowship with His Father. The world should likewise know our God connection, in the same way by the lives we live in Christ.

17: 22

And the glory which thou gavest me, I have given them; that they may be one, even as we are one.

As Jesus continues to pray to the Father, he now declares he would give his saints honor, (*glory*) as he was given by the Father, and that they would be in union and harmony and one in the Spirit as they were. This was not being asked said because any of them, or us deserves it. It was done as an act of completion.

The disciples were a part of a spiritual circle, united with the Father, Son, and the Holy Spirit. Here Jesus is speaking in past tense. He was talking about something he shared with his Father always. This glory he spoke of was always his from before the foundation of the world, as he speaks of in another verse.

Being one with the Father and Son has a requirement that must be made, and what it that? To be obedient. Everything Jesus is saying in this prayer is focused on being, and remaining connected in spiritual harmony with God.

17: 23

I in them and thou in me, that they may be perfect in one; and that the world may know that thou hast sent me, and hast loved them, as thou hast loved me.

Together we form a more perfect union, Father, Son, Spirit, and believers, all working, moving and thinking as one.

Jesus said to be perfect as our Father in heaven is perfect (*Matthew 5: 48*). Perfect being complete or mature, *teleios*. This maturity is part of the growth process that every believer goes through coming into the body of Christ through salvation.

The Apostle Paul put it this way: when I was a child I spoke as a child, I understood as a child, I thought as a child, but when I became a man, (*grew up*) I put away childish things (*I Corinthians 13: 12*).

This perfection comes once we are rooted and built up in Christ and established in the faith (*Colossians 2: 7*).

God's love is perfected in us as we show love one for another (*I John 4: 12*).

We are God's little children and have overcome the spirit of Antichrist that is filling the world, our victory is our faith, (*I John 5: 4*). Jesus said His sheep hear His voice and will not follow another. In fact, they will flee from the strangers voice, (*John 10: 1-5*).

Even as the world is sinful and full of wickedness, Christ is still reaching out to the lost. Jesus prays that the world would know that He was sent by God to save them from the penalty that has been brought on by sin.

Jesus' prayer was that the unsaved would come to know how much they were loved by God. This can only be done by those who know and show God's love in a tangible way.

The world cannot see God, but they can see us. Those of us who have called on the Lord must depart from iniquity (*II Timothy 2: 19*), and let the light of the Lord burn so brightly that they, the lost can see our good works and glorify, give honor to God (*Matthew 5: 16*).

17: 24

Father I will that they also, whom thou hast given me, be where I am; that they might behold your glory, that which thou hast given me: for thou lovest me before the foundation of the world.

Jesus request was that the Father would let the disciples be with Him where He was from, that is Heaven. This is a very specific request. Jesus' words were, "Father I pray" that they also be where I am.

God would honor them. In fact, they (the Apostles) would sit down with Christ in His kingdom, they would sit on thrones judging the twelve tribes of Israel as God has appointed them (*Luke 22: 29, 30*).

When James and John asked that they be allowed to sit on Jesus' right and left hand when He came into His glory (*Mark 10: 35-40*), they had no idea what it was they were truly asking. Like so many today we can say things but not actually take into consideration what the consequences of what we ask might be. Jesus let them know that that appointment of seating was in his Fathers hands.

James and John were seeking these positions selfishly and even caused some resentment from the other disciples, (*v.41*), most likely because they felt they were close to Christ because they were a part of what would later be called the inner circle.

In the body of Christ, we do not go where we want to go, we are placed where we will give God the greatest glory, we are placed where it pleases Him.

For the body is not one member, but many.

If the foot shall say, Because I am not the hand, I am not of the body; is it therefore not of the body?

And if the ear shall say, Because I am not the eye, I am not of the body; is it therefore not of the body?

If the whole body were an eye, where were the hearing? If the whole were hearing, where were the smelling?

But now hath God set the members every one of them in the body, as it hath pleased him. - I Corinthians 12: 14-18

Jesus wanted them, (*those who walked with him, and those who would come to know him later*) all to experience His glory (*Honor*) as three of them had done so on the mountain (*Luke 9: 28-35*).

John tells us that they had beheld His glory as the only begotten Son, (*John 1: 14*).

Jesus' prayer was also in the future tense, and the words he spoke would cover even the believers today.

17: 25

O righteous Father, the world has not known thee: but I have known thee, and these have known that thou hast sent me.

There are people who call themselves spiritual, people who have a form of godliness, but not according to knowledge.

The fear, (*respect, reverence*) of God, we are told is the beginning of knowledge, but fools despise wisdom and instruction (**Proverbs 1:7**).

We are told that God is a righteous Father, a father who loves His children will always seek and do what is best for them.

The Lord will bless the righteous (**Psalm 5: 12**), and His judgments are upright (**Psalm 119: 137**) and His commandments are faithful (**v.138**).

The Lord said that He would raise unto David, a righteous Branch; and a King that shall reign and prosper, and execute judgment and justice on earth, (**Jeremiah 23: 5**).

This Branch is the Lord's Christ, who would come out of the stem of Jesse's roots, (*David's Father by birth*), and the spirit of the Lord shall rest upon Him, (**Isaiah 11: 1-5**), read carefully what Jesus said as He entered His ministry. *The Spirit of the Lord is upon me, because he hath anointed me to preach the gospel to the poor; he hath sent me to heal the brokenhearted, to preach deliverance to the captives, and recovering of sight to the blind, to set at liberty them that are bruised,*

To preach the acceptable year of the Lord.

And he closed the book, and he gave it again to the minister, and sat down. And the eyes of all them that were in the synagogue were fastened on him.

And he began to say unto them, This day is this scripture fulfilled in your ears. (*Luke 4: 18-21*).

The world could not see or accept the righteousness of God. All those who come to God, must believe that He is, and that He is the rewarder of them that diligently seek Him, (*Hebrews 11: 6*).

Who God is, becomes clear to us the moment we experience the power of his grace by the Holy Spirit. Paul said, we have been looking in a glass darkly, not seeing things clearly, but soon we will understand them once we are face to face with the Lord (*I Corinthians 13: 12*).

The saints do not have a problem accepting the person of Jesus Christ as God's Son sent into the world, rejected of man, (*Matthew 21: 42; Mark chapter 1- 2: 10; Luke 20: 17*), who died on a cross; being raised from the dead, and is now seated at the right hand of the Father, (*Romans 8: 4; Hebrews 1: 3*). This is where every saint hope rests.

17: 26

And I have declared unto them thy name, and will declare it: that the love wherewith thou hast loved me may be in them, and I in them.

Jesus was concluding one of the most powerful prayers to his Father and the disciples were blessed to hear it even though they did not understand its meaning at that moment.

Jesus came to make the name of the Father known in the world of sin; the world would reject His claim to be the Son of God, and would have Him crucified for making such a statement. And even though he would be crucified for his doctrine he knew it was the only way to redeem mankind.

It would be God who had a group of selected men, He had chosen, that would tell the world of a new covenant that Jesus was establishing in the world.

Jesus had made known His Father's name and will to those He had chosen, sanctified, and ordained, and would continue to do so by the ministering power of the Holy Spirit until he was crucified, died, raised from the dead, and ascended back to Heaven.

Jesus would soon be arrested and tried by sinful men who were not faithful to the scriptures through willful disobedience.

This prayer of Jesus puts the light on the type of relationship Christ Jesus had with His Father in every way, from eternity to eternity. This is the bond that Jesus prayed each of His disciples would enjoy with Him.

Jesus was focused on having the disciples know the God of creation in a very personal way, to experience His power, His majesty, and His glory like no human being has ever done.

This would be a time that the disciples could experience heaven on earth, and to understand what Jesus meant when He said the Kingdom of Heaven is within. Amen and Amen.

Closing Thought

How you come to the Lord is not anyone's business, but it is important that you do.

And the Spirit and the Bride say, Come. And let Him that Hears say Come. And let Him who is thirsty come.

And whosoever will, let them come and take of the water of life freely

*(**Revelation 22:17**)*.

Some Simple Prayers

I do not have control of my life; I give my heart to you and surrender my will to yours.

I want to know you and the power of your Son Jesus.

Thank you Lord for sending your Son Jesus Christ to die for me.

Wash me and cleanse me of my sins.

Forgive me my rebellion against you.

I confess my sins to you Father and accept Jesus' death and resurrection, come into my life.

Lord have mercy on me, a sinner.

Lord save me.

Conclusion

God does not look on the outward appearance, but He judges the intent of the Heart. All that call upon the Lord (*sincerely*) shall be saved (***Romans.10: 13***).

About the Author

Timothy White Sr. has impacted thousands of people throughout the world as an author, teacher, motivational speaker and minister. Mr. White is on a mission to positively influence millions of people through his work, ministry and writing, which currently exceeds 80+ books covering a plethora of topics including bullying, domestic violence, self-help, history and spirituality.

The Cleveland, Ohio native, a father of five, has overcome many adversities in his life including homelessness and losing his beloved wife to cancer in 1994. Through much heartache and disappointments he discovered a new purpose and passion to use writing as a tool to "plant positive seeds."

Mr. White has developed profound spiritual insight into relationships over the years. Mr. White has written multiple books on the topic of abuse including, *In the Ring with Heels On*, *She's the Boss and Victims of Bullies*. Mr. White writes about these and other issues because of the relevance, and prevalence of domestic and other violence. He believes that, **"Information plus application equals transformation."**

Mr. White is an Evangelist and former pastor. He believes, "God chooses who He uses." He writes, speaks, and ministers to local, national, and international audiences. With an additional 15 new books in the works, Mr. White hopes to give people plenty of "spiritual food" to eat.

White is one of the producers of the documentary ***"Where's Gina?"*** about missing children on which he was also narrator.

He is a co-developer of a tech company (Gsys LLC) that brought blindside technology to vehicles that made billions for the industry, saving countless lives. He is currently co-hosting a radio show, *"Healing the Hurt"* on WERE 1490am in Cleveland, Ohio on Thursday evenings 8-10 pm with Host, Rev. Brenda Ware-Abrams.

He is currently on the Advisory Board and is a volunteer instructor at the Juvenile Correction centers in Warrensville Heights and Cleveland, Ohio where his book *Seven Signs of Success* is being taught. His book *Victims of Bullies* is, currently, in the City of Cleveland School system to help stop and make aware of solutions to the issue of bullying.

timwhite55@gmail.com   Timwhitepublishing.com

www.ingramcontent.com/pod-product-compliance
Lightning Source LLC
Chambersburg PA
CBHW031225090426
42740CB00007B/714